Autographs

POCKET KNOWLEDGE

(12x20 Keys To Great Leadership)

By Denaryle Lovell Williams

San Marcos California, 2015

Dedication

This book is primarily dedicated to all the young people out there who need guidance and true leadership development. In addition this book is also dedicated to the many adults I've observed who were not properly trained on how to become effective leaders. I have an obligation as a mentor, life coach, and leader to share all the knowledge and experience I have gained over the years so that it can help the leaders of today become the great leaders of tomorrow.

This book is also dedicated to my family who has always supported me in my many endeavors. To my mother Dorothy O Williams; I appreciate all the strong advice you have given me over the years and your continual strong stands to this day. I developed a strong sense of who I

*was created to be because you pushed me
into leadership at a very young age.
Thank you so much and I love you even
though we are two strong leaders and
clash most of the time because we are
that way! Lol… To my sister Dene: I
am so glad that we were allowed to
experience all that we did as children
both good and bad because it made us
who we are today. You too are a great
leader and have greatness inside waiting
to explode. Look out world because when
she finally comes forward it will be
powerful! To my niece Secara, CEO of
Perfecting Image Photography and
Graphic Design; you too are a great
leader and very talented person that I
have had the privilege to help to
nurture. Thank you for all that you have
done for all my projects including this
one. I love and appreciate you so much!
To My nephews De'Aer, Justus, and*

J'Airus; I as your Uncle D have always strived to be the best example of a man and leader for you to exhibit. I know how it feels to not have your dad around and that is why I always put you first and sacrificed as much as I did so you would know how to walk in true responsibility, great leadership and become strong black men. To EJ, Saniyah, Aanyah and my little nephew Lil EEJ; I also dedicate this book to you. Anything I do to leave my mark on this world will always be dedicated to my family. A wise man leaves a legacy for his children's children and I want to be known as a wise man. This includes my Grandmother Lucy B. Williams, and all my great aunts; who are all blessed to see over 85 years on this earth as of the writing of this book in 2014.

*To Pastor's Robert E. Joyce, the late
Laverne O. Joyce and Michael Jones;
thank you for your obedience in seeing
the gifting inside of me and helping to
cultivate it. Thank you also for being
great examples of leadership and
pushing me to be the leader I am today.*

*Last but certainly not least I thank God
for the ability he has given me to
articulate through words, inspire, and
encourage people through such a gift as
writing. I am forever grateful for this
ability and talent that I have been
blessed to share with the world.*

Epigraph

Leadership and development of leaders is a very important part of who I am. I have spent the better part of 20 years leading and developing leaders. Through the avenue of education and sports I can proudly say I have help to develop thousands of leaders up to date. I can honestly say it has been a privilege working to foster leadership and develop tomorrow's leaders. This has been my mantra and motivation for years and I pray that these words encourage all who read this book. "The ability to bring out the best in individuals is an art. With God's help I have succeeded in doing so. I strive to bring out the best in others while being the best myself. If one were to ask me what I think of myself? I will tell you I am exactly who and what God says that I am, and I will always tell others that exact same thing!"

-Denaryle Lovell Williams

POCKET KNOWLEDGE

(12x20 Keys To Great Leadership)

Contents

Quotes by Denaryle Lovell Williams

Leadership

"Leadership is developed over years!"

"Leadership is refined through life's challenges!"

"Leadership is solidified through acceptance of one's individual destiny!"

"Leadership is qualified by those who have walked in true leadership and recognize up and coming leaders!"

"Leadership is justified by the actions of he or she who truly walks as a great leader!"

Never Be Content

"Never be content with someone's definition of you, instead define yourself by your own truths, by your own beliefs, by your own morals, by your own personal convictions, and by your unique understanding of who you are and how you have come to be. Never be contented until you are happy with the inimitable individual God created you to be from the very day of your existence!"

Identity

I define who I am!

I define what I stand for!

I decide how far I will go in life!

I make the choice to be great in my own right!

I will not let anyone define me!

I will not let small minded people determine my potential, latitude or altitude!

I will always be mindful of my confessions over my life and future!

I am the executer of my destiny!

I will speak positively over myself knowing that I am only as great as my last confession!

I will not be limited by cynical professions over me!

I will collide head on with my destiny!

I will help others define themselves!

"I will reach my full potential simply because I know who I am!

Forward thinking

"True leaders Lead from the front!"

"True leaders are not looking for a place to belong they create places where others belong!"

"True leaders are never caught by surprise they surprise others by always being prepared!"

"True leaders are never reactive they are constantly proactive!"

"True leaders critically think, think confidently, think ahead, think before they speak, and rarely over think!"

"True leaders create leaders around them!"

"True leaders are thermostats not thermometers; they never adjust to their environments they create them!

"

NO MORE BOXES!

We wake up in a box!

We clean up in a box!

We look in a box to prepare ourselves for the day!

We eat in and at a box!

We travel in a box!

We are educated while sitting at a box as the teacher instructs from a box!

We learn, work, matriculate, and graduate from a box, to later have a career in a box!

We text, call, and social network from a box!

We spend a lot of time watching and being entertained by a box!

We live most of our lives in boxes but yet are taught to think outside of the box!

Why should we expect anything more than the compartmentalized mental captivity that lies within a boxed way of thinking?

It is impossible to expect a leader to emerge outside of the normal existence of boxes, but great leaders grow beyond expectancy from others!

True leaders live outside the box while rebelling against the stagnation of boxes created to diminish our mental capacity!

True leader see the box as an opportunity to excel beyond expectation!

A good leader uses the box to defy the odds that lie within that boxes limitation!

A great leader says 'nothing will stop them from obtaining greatness, freedom, and liberation!"

NO MORE BOXES!

Introduction -

As a mentor, educator and coach for twenty years I was compelled to write this book on leadership. As a life coach today I feel compelled to motivate people as I witness the decline in leadership today. With the increase of social networks and the decrease of verbal communication amongst people I feel it necessary to address this subject. The basis of this book contains nuggets of information that will help to develop the leader within. Leadership is something that is developed and cultivated within a person primarily through experience. One of the most effective ways of leadership development is through observation. For many years I was

privileged to have great leaders
lead by example. It is from this
type of leadership style that I
developed the leader within.

The purpose of this
book is to show the reader very
practical ways to develop and
cultivate their leadership skills. My
goal is to leave the reader excited
about their potential as a leader.
One of the things I have heard over
the years is that young people are
the leaders of tomorrow and I
bought into this for a while but not
so much now. I believe leaders are
developed long before we actually
see the attributes of such
leadership. The longer we put off
developing our young people's
leadership skills the longer it takes
for them to walk confidently in

such leadership. When I was an impressionable young man the number one leader in my life was a Pastor who had no problem tapping into my leadership. On many occasions he took the liberty of putting me up on different platforms weather I was ready or not. I thought he was crazy most of the time because this came very spontaneously. However, what it did was kept me in a mindset of constantly being ready to perform sort of speak. The definition of faux pas is an embarrassing or tactless act or remark in a social situation. This happened to me only a few times as the spontaneity kept me well prepared for the unexpected. I look back at this now and realize that this made my leadership even stronger because it allowed me freedom weather prepared or not so prepared to speak at any given time or situation. I would like to publicly thank Robert Joyce for such preparation as it has put me in many great positions to speak and develop others leadership.

I came up with the name "Pocket Knowledge" because I wanted something small and efficient enough for a person to carry around in their pocket to refer to at any given time or situation. It is with this inkling that this book was created. As an educator for the last twenty years or so I am more and more convinced that we are not preparing our students with the knowledge they need to be great leaders. I have observed over the years a structure become an educational system that is more excited about test scores and not concerned about critical thinking skills. Education today has stolen the creativity of students and replaced it with this notion that all students learn exactly the same which is completely preposterous. I for one think that this style of education is stealing precious knowledge from our youth, and learners of all ages who have to endure this type of education. It is as if we are now producing students like they are on a manufacturing assembly line or something.   In addition to this teachers are no longer being graded for their example as a hardworking, caring educator but how high their student's test scores are, coupled with harsh criticisms and reprimands if their students have low test scores. We have moved away from very basic leadership and character development to this machine that we call common education. We were introduced to "No child left behind" and now are being forced to endure "common core" education which came in a very discrete and mischievous manner. Sure enough there is some good in both but the core of these curriculums fail miserably at creating leaders as a whole. Most people don't even realize that "common core" did not come from the department of education but through other means, ideas, and people with financial influence. I encourage any and all who read this book to research and find out exactly where it came from!

As a leader and educator it saddens me to see our young people deprived of some of the very foundational aspects of education I received.   The sad reality is that we can give a young person an electronic device and they can do anything but if you take away such devices they would be lost. I am further convinced that we have moved away from true leadership development and have become crutches in a plethora of ways. If I were to compare our country to other countries and even my interactions with foreign students it is very obvious that our emphasis on basic skill development has diminished drastically. Some of the very foundational habits and character building exercises of old that I see in students of other countries has become hidden in political correctness in this country. In our efforts to not offend or be confrontational we have lost some very basic skills that our young people will never experience. So therefore, it is with this experience and observation that I have written this book. I am encouraged by this book and hope that it helps everyone who obtains it to become a better more effective leader.

POCKET KNOWLEDGE

(12x20 Keys To Great Leadership)

Chapter One

Intrinsic qualities of a great leader

POCKET KNOWLEDGE
12x20 Keys To Great Leadership

I as an author, mentor, and life coach often ask myself the question; am I doing enough as a leader of leader's? As a former educator frustrated with my job I left feeling like I was rendered helpless because of the manner in which education forced us to teach with little opportunity to lead by example. I watched daily as teachers became more and more frustrated with their jobs as their ability to be free and to teach freely was taken away by blanket formats that we call new methods. Leadership to me is a person making a choice to allow their lives to be an example to others and this is what I remember about my teachers, adults as well as leaders I respected and looked up to. Sure times have changed but one fact still remains and that is that we must teach our youth to be leaders!

In this chapter I will highlight many attributes that can be found in a great leader. The person who possesses these qualities tends to be the ones who are considered great leaders. The following list of attributes are external and not innate qualities that one is typically born with. They are developed over time in a surfeit of ways. They could be mimicked, taught, duplicated through strong mentorship, leadership or simply refined purposely for building ones outgoing persona.

The idea of this knowledge is to equip the individual reading this book with tools that enhances their leadership ability. I truly want the average person to possess these qualities so that they are always prepared for and in any situation. My hope is that this knowledge can be used to create those leaders of tomorrow. With this knowledge we can move beyond the non- critical thinking aspects of education today back to good old information that helps people to move forward.

Attributes of Great Leadership

Honesty – The person who is honest and up right with those they encounter are truly those who have the purest intentions. Honesty is a great quality to possess when leading or aspiring to be a leader. The definition of honesty; - fairness and straightforwardness of conduct. This means that one is conscious of his or her conduct always being straight forward in speech and deed. Honesty is truly the best policy of a great leader!

Integrity- The person who has integrity is one who purposely walks in and with the highest level of character.

This person is cognizant of their reputation and protects it with the accompanying actions. The definition of integrity is: firm adherence to a code of especially moral or artistic values, the quality or state of being complete or undivided. The person who walks in integrity has strong values and never deviates from such values.

Morality- The term "morality" can be used either descriptively to refer to some codes of conduct put forward by a society or some other group, such as a religion, or accepted by an individual for their own behavior or normatively to refer to a code of conduct that, given specified conditions, would be put forward by all rational persons. Morality is another great attribute to possess as a leader because it allows the leader to be fair in all his or her actions. The person with moral conviction will never walk in a waivered disposition because they stand firm in their moral principles.

Stability- To have stability as a leader means that this person is firmly set in place weather in speech, or action. One must be stable mentally and physically to walk in great leadership. The person with stability never vacillates in their decision making and is not considered an irresolute individual. They stand firm and confident in their overall disposition as a leader.

Loquacious- The one who has great communication skills and effective communication tactics will be a successful leader. When a leader cannot properly or clearly communicate it hinders their ability as a leader to effectively lead. This type of leader is not afraid to speak in any given situation. It is important that a leader practices great communication skills both vocal and written to be the best leader he or she can be.

Patient- To walk in patience additionally is also a great quality to have as a leader. This allows the leader to have empathy and care for those he or she may be leading. There is a popular saying that is as follows; "patience is a virtue" and this virtue goes along way when leading or being led. The leader who is patient and has taken the time to develop patience will never make hasty or regretful decisions.

Persistent- The leader who is persistent is one who will never quit, give up in any situation or circumstance. This attribute is accompanied with a stick-to-itiveness and strong determination to not give up. This attribute is pivotal as it is constantly needed for progression, possession, innovation, and achievement. As a leader it is important to remember that persistence pays off!

Confident- The one who is confident possesses an attitude of assurance that is not shaken by external circumstances. By definition confidence is; a feeling or belief that you can do something well or succeed at something, a feeling or belief that someone or something is good or has the ability to succeed at something. I live by the saying; "to an insecure person a confident person will always appear arrogant!" With this attribute it is very easy to mistake confidence for arrogance, but true confidence is rarely seen by those who are not confident themselves and one should not be ashamed of being confident.

Dedicated- The person who is dedicated possesses a deep commitment to seeing a task or project through to its completion. This commitment is not limited to a project but also people and causes typically dear to the leader's heart. Definition: a feeling of very strong support for or loyalty to someone or something: the quality or state of being dedicated to a person, group, cause, etc. This particular trait seems to be lost in this generation and it is vital for any leader to possess this missing trait essential to great leadership.

Motivated- The person who is motivated needs no inspiration from others to perform any given task. This is not to be mistaken as saying that they are not inspired by others. This simply means that they have found a way to stay motivated and are continually up for any task given to them. The leader who is motivated typically is just as great at motivating others to action. The leader who is motivated is quickly and greatly inspired and rarely needs incentive from others to move to action.

Audacity- This word is synonymous with nerve and courage so it is somewhat misleading. The person with this attribute is one who will step out and lead no matter what the cost. They embody bravery and courage that has been developed through experience and life lessons. It is rare but not uncommon to see this in leaders without this being developed. Some are born with a natural audacity and function very well in it. This like many attributes this must be balanced with other skills to be affective as this type of nerve can be intimidating to those who don't walk in it naturally.

Secure- The person who possesses this attribute is one who is comfortable with themselves. They have worked on who they are, and typically are not moved by what others try to say that they are or should be. Security is huge because as a leader you must have a strong foundation and not be easily persuaded. This is not to say that there are not areas in our lives where we are most vulnerable, but a great leader does not let it bring about torpor. A great leader must walk confidently and not insecurely at all times.

It is so critical that a person's character is dominated with these types of qualities. Life coaches, mentors, and others like myself play a huge role in developing these attributes. However, no greater responsibility supersedes that of the preparation one receives from home training. This is the reason this book was not only geared towards our youth but anyone including parents, and any other adults who never had the opportunity to be properly trained as a leader. I feel very strongly that somewhere along the way we have lost the very vital nurturing of these intrinsic qualities. The reassuring part is that this book along with many other great examples of leadership guidance will help the next generation become those nurtured individuals who have had the opportunity, exampling, and assurance they need to walk in leadership roles.

When I first introduced this book I spoke on the importance of leadership not only for this generation but also for the former generations who never had the opportunity to be properly trained on how to walk in true leadership. Now to some this may seem crazy but there are many individuals out there who never had anyone to show them how to be leaders. They were never given an opportunity to be introduced to literature or written materials that would help them become leaders. Finally some even for social and economic reasons were never given the resources to become positive and effective leaders. This resulting in poor exampling or the lack of leaders completely. For this and many other reasons I have written this book and given these very critical steps for both youth and adults of all ages to be the beneficiaries.

With these very critical qualities one can move forward both in confidence and well equipped to handle any situation that comes their way. The qualities of a great leader are shown through their character and what has been carefully developed over time. One is at his or her best when they exhibit such qualities and they leave a very distinctive impression on those they come into contact with. This is very important because first impressions are lasting, and you never get a second opportunity to make a first impression. One would be advantageous to do this correct the first time and utilize all the information given so that they may be successful.

Chapter Two

Physiognomies of great leaders

Who we are as people is often dictated by those whom we spend the most time with. For many years I have mentored individuals who have had a certain mindset. As I continued in this role I realized that the little time I spent with different individuals was nothing compared to the lifetime they had with friends, family, and other influences both good and bad. I finally realized that I could not take it personal when I didn't effect these individuals right away, instead I had to look at this as a role I played in the village in preparing these individuals for life. So I took advantage of the time I did have and focused on their overall success. This would carry over into their lives beyond their time with me because the village is forever and I am just a contributor of the village!

The following lists of physiognomies that I will describe; stand out, and are specific to ones over all persona or MO. The term MO-Modus operandi (often used in the abbreviated form MO) is a Latin phrase, approximately translated as "mode of operation." The plural is modi operandi ("modes of operation"). It is used in police work to describe a criminal's characteristic, patterns and style of work. The reason I chose to use this terminology is because I feel that it's okay that one possesses a positive MO. In detective work it is used to describe a person's mode of operations, so I figured I could use it as a determining factor to describe the character of a leader and their mode of operation. When a person very carefully and purposely works on their character and persona it should be known as the way that they are or conduct themselves constantly. This is in no way a bad thing but establishes who a person really is.

As you the partaker of this knowledge began an encirclement of these different characteristics my hope is that you can benefit from this information. I further hope that this allows room for you the reader to grow and apply such knowledge to enhance your skill levels. Finally that you will practice such skills to become a great leader while teaching others to lead. All the while doing so with the same passion and desire that you have obtained by leading with and through example.

Here are the physiognomies that were elected purposely and specifically for this book;

A *great follower*- The person who aspires to be a leader must first be a great follower. Leadership is misunderstood in many ways because people don't realize that great leaders were once great followers who paid very close attention to their leaders. Great followers learn from both good and bad leaders to develop their strong leadership style. Typically those who don't like to follow become unsuccessful leaders as they have missed some very key education on becoming a great leader. A great follower is not to be mistaken for any reason. Those who are great followers learn essential qualities that are apparent in their leadership panache.

Verbal- One of the main characteristics of a great leader is his or her ability to be talkative. They must embody the ability to talk to anyone in any given situation. They have to possess great communicating skills and be able to properly and effectively communicate to and for those around them.

Attentive- This distinguishing trait is a must for any great leader. It is absolutely imperative that a leader be completely aware of their surroundings. The ability for a great leader to be observant is key to their success as a leader. When you as a leader are aware of everything that surrounds you it keeps you completely sensitive to your immediate as well as outer surroundings.

Stand Out- this characteristic is one that is a compliment to any great leader. As a leader you should always be one who stands out. You should be noticed and take notice of any situation that needs a stand out to lead. This type of leader cannot hide they are easily noticed, and not afraid to step up, out or move forward.

Competitive- The leader who possesses this characteristic is one who through very intelligent choices moves aggressively towards situations. This characteristic can be misleading because people with competitive natures in most cases are negatively aggressive. They tend to only look out for themselves while hating to lose however, when used in the proper manner a competitive oriented person such as a great leader will not come off negatively but as a person who is a go getter.

Tenacious- The leader who possesses this characteristic is diligent and will not give up. They are resolute and stands firm in their positioning and never settles for less than the overall outcome they are trying to achieve.

Empathetic- The leader who exhibits this type of quality in their character is one who is in tune with those around them. They have the ability to be sympathetic and can empathize with others.

Cognizant- any great leader is totally and completely aware of his or her surroundings at all times. In addition to their surroundings they are also aware of any potential situations that may occur in any way. *This* characteristic is very necessary as a leader to equip any leader so that they are never caught by surprise.

Accommodating- Any great leader always wants to be known as one who is helpful to others around them. To be accepting of others is not only what we all should do as people but it is very necessary for one who aspires to be a great leader. This one is very important as it protects both a leader and potential interactions with people from any form of conflict or complaint. A great leader recognizes that everyone has needs physically, emotionally, and psychologically as such needs are particular and specific to every individual.

Performs tasks with excellence- I have always said "that there is a big difference between excellence and perfection!" When a leader can distinguish the difference between the two they will never be constrained to being and doing things perfectly. No man is perfect so we can only do the best that we are capable of doing. When a leader understands this then they will never operate under the pressure of being and performing perfectly. This leader has a clear understanding of the difference between doing things to the best of their ability verses doing things perfectly. When any tasks are performed with excellence the leader can walk away knowing they have done the best job possible they are capable of doing. However, when there is a misnomer that things can be done perfectly and when they aren't the leader leaves feeling like they have failed. This is why it is indicative for the leader to always function with excellence in everything they do.

Not insecure- I cannot express how important it is for a great leader to not function in insecurity. It would be foolish of me to say that we as leaders are not insecure in one way or the other, but what I am speaking of is insecurity as a whole. The insecure leader will never be confident in his or her decisions, choices, actions, or functionality. Any issues of insecurity must be met head on and settled in order for a great leader to function without this fear. There are many ways to overcome insecurity but one must first know beyond a shadow of a doubt who they are and what their purpose is in life. This will allow the leader to be secure in their mission which leaves little room for questioning one's self.

A duplicator of one's self Any great leader must not be afraid of duplicating themselves. This is almost impossible not to do as a leader is constantly being watched and followed. The insecure leader will never allow their self to be duplicated as they are afraid that they will lose their position over someone or something. The insecure leader has to have a hand on or over people they are intimidated by. However, a secure leader has no problem sharing who they are, their strengths, their talents, as well as their failures to better those around them. Duplication is a true attribute of a great leader as those around them choose to mimic the leader's behavior as a compliment of their great leadership. Never forget that imitation is the highest form of flattery!

Takes risks- A great leader is never afraid to do something different. They have an inner strength that allows them to be fearless to a certain extent. They move quickly to explore a new adventure without apprehension. They are willing to take risks knowing what it entails. Finally they live by the saying; "to go somewhere you have never gone you must do something you have never done!"

Not afraid to be stretched- Any good leader understands that to become better they will encounter obstacles that will stretch them. To be stretched means to be put to the test in many ways. This will put you in uncomfortable situations that will take you beyond what you may think your breaking point is. The end result is character being built through this period. To be stretched is to be put into very unusual and unique situations that result in your maturity as a leader. This also prepares you as the leader to assist others. As everyone who aspires to become a leader will encounter similar situations. Such situations you were once in you can now be of assistance to help others through.

A trail blazer-True leaders are trail blazers not path finders. Great leaders are always looking for a path to create. They choose not to follow paths already created but are unique enough to find their own way or trail to blaze. There is a saying that goes like this; "don't re-invent the wheel" which typically means not to do something that is already done for you but true leaders are sharp enough to know when to work smarter not harder. They can discern when they need to create such paths that should be followed versus utilizing those paths that are beneficial to both them and those that they lead.

Listens well- One of the true marks of a great leader is one who listens well. In any successful communication it takes both speaking and listening however, listening is the most crucial part of any level of communication. Listening is a true leadership quality that is perfected while building relationship with those around you. The ability to recognize that everyone needs a sounding board every now and again is important. Always remember that you as a great leader are privileged to provide disciplined listening for those in need, and is paramount in your leadership persona.

Approachable- Another great mark of a good leader is his or her ability to be available for those that need them. A leader should always be willing to be contacted by others. A leader should never get so big that they are no longer approachable. An insecure leader never allows people to get close to them. There is that very thin balance between allowing people to get close that never grow from the close contact and that leader who assumes all people are leeches. The approachable leader is also well exercised in discernment. This allows them to know the difference between a time bandit and one who truly needs their attention. Like anything there is a balance in everything we do as leaders so in being approachable don't be over whelmed to the point that you are non-effective.

Not arrogant- I live by the saying; "to an insecure person a confident person will always appear arrogant!" *True* confidence is rarely recognized and always mistaken for arrogance. The insecure leader displays a need to be seen, heard, and from a distance seemingly in control but never truly secure in their self. The leader who is arrogant hides behind their lack of confidence in themselves. There is nothing ever wrong with being confident it is contagious if duplicated correctly. Confidence reproduces more confidence however, arrogance releases insecurity and a false sense of security to those in the company of an arrogant leader. Stay away from this type of leadership and become a confident leader.

Optimistic- the leader who is encouraging is never seen as a negative person. They always see the cup as half full and never looking at situations with or through a negative light. They are great to be around because they bring a positive vibe and or energy while creating an environment of possibilities. This leader is not unrealistic in any way they make a choice to see things through a progressive light. This type of leader understands that they gage the temperature for those around them and choose to keep it consistent with optimism.

A great visionary- One of the ultimate marks of a great leader is their ability to be filled with vision. They are not only one who envisions what they want but they can communicate such visions to those around them. This type of leader is always pregnant with the next thing to deliver. They remain healthy while surrounding themselves with like- minded people. The visionary is never lost as they typically go from vision to vision. They are never disappointed by something that may not come to fruition because they remain constantly full of vision. More than the leader being a great visionary it is very important for them to effectively deliver this vision so that others not only understand it but can efficiently execute such vision.

So there you have it the twenty characteristics of a great leader. I purposely used the word characteristic because it denotes something that has been worked on to perfection. A person's over all persona and identity is developed through much experience and growth. When one who aspires to be a leader has taken the time and effort to work on such crucial improvements of their character they are showing how important this development truly is.

A person's character is who they are and not something they are trying to be. One of my favorite sayings is as follows; "reputation is what people think you are, but character is what you truly possess!" So with this statement I want to make it clear that your character as a leader is very important and should never be taken lightly. As leaders we have a duty to present ourselves appropriately and without flaw. Please don't misunderstand the term flaw as me saying we are incapable of making mistakes because we will and do. What I am saying is that one who works on his or her character and truly have pure intentions will be as flawless as they can be. I can't be everyone else but I sure can be who I truly am! Denaryle Lovell Williams and this is advice I now pass on to you the reader.

As I stated earlier in the book imitation is the highest form of flattery so when bidding others compliments be sure to remember that you are your own person and not some cheap imitation of someone else. This is why we work on our character and perfect our own personas. This allows us to be unique, exceptional, idealistic, opportunistic, and unscrupulous individuals that have our own distinct nature.

I was inspired to write this poem after completing this chapter. I am always willing to encourage and foster one being an individual unique to his or herself. I hope it inspires you as the reader to do so!

Check out this inspiration on the next page!!!

Yes I Am My Own Person!

I am an individual who was created to be me and only me.

I was not an afterthought that reflects a cheap imitation of someone else.

I am unique in nature, stature, physical qualities, and identity.

I am comfortable in my own skin and understand that I was created this way for a reason and purpose idiosyncratic to my own individuality.

*I daily choose to work on my
character and perfect my inimitable
persona.*

*I am cognizant of the work it
takes to become great in my own
right and mind.*

*This sets me a part from the
rest, and establishes who I am.*

*It helps to cement me into
my extraordinary identifying
qualities.*

*Which inevitably assists me
in having my own distinct nature.*

*I am transformed daily
mentally and physically because of
the conscious decisions I make to
remain grounded.*

*When I put this all together
it allows me to be unique,
exceptional, idealistic,
opportunistic, and an unscrupulous
individual.*

Yes I Am My Own Person!

Chapter Three

Evolution from follower to leader

POCKET KNOWLEDGE
12x20 Keys To Great Leadership

It is amazing how many people choose to take the back seat when it comes to Leadership. I have purposed in my heart to never negate an opportunity to take the lead. It is vital that those who desire to move forward in leadership to do so with confidence and boldness. It is not always easy to step up and be the one who decides to lead however, with a little help anyone can do it. I wanted to leave you with these steps or stages it takes to lead successfully. These are my own steps but they have proven to be very valuable in my maturation into leadership.

Baby Steps; just like a small child who must first learn how to crawl the aspiring leader must crawl before they walk. Many people have taken on roles of leadership that they were not properly prepared for which resulted in failure. The leader who takes the time and effort to perfect their leadership skills and abilities is the intelligent leader who inevitably becomes a successful leader. One should never rush into leadership without first being a successful follower who enjoyed every aspect of following. The successful follower has taken the necessary steps to be a successful leader.

The courage it takes to lead; Leadership is not always as easy as it looks. The person(s) we see in leadership roles have gone through a process of overcoming certain fears. Many people fear speaking in front of crowds of people, certain physical enablement, becoming a social blunder, fear of failing, or fear of rejection. Courage is something that is embraced and taken on as one's character. Courage is needed in order to face some of the challenges of leadership. It takes a lot of courage to step up and out into the forefront of any role that a leader takes. The courage it takes to lead is something that a great leader must develop and become very comfortable possessing. Courage chokes out fear, anxiety and empowers the leader to lead with confidence.

Next is *making up your mind to lead;* the up and coming leader can possess all the information they need to be a leader however, if they are not mentally ready to walk in such leadership then they will fail. The potential leader must have his or her mind made up that they not only want to lead but they can lead. If the mental sovereignty is not there then there will be an uneasiness that paralyzes the leader mentally. This issue must be settled first and expeditiously so the leader can walk in full mental freedom and confidence.

Walking away from being a follower; the up and coming leader understands that they are constantly walking but now have the opportunity to walk away from following into leading. To walk away from something means you are walking into something else. So as the leader is exercising faith in their abilities to lead they are taking advantage of the opportunity to be a leader while letting the role of follower go. It is important that the up and coming leader understands that you never walk completely away from following. A great follower will always be a greater leader, but we all follow from time to time and in certain capacities. It keeps us humble, consistent, and is a constant reminder of what we have accomplished as well as where we have come from. Never forget that the way one exits a situation is the way that they will enter a new situation so always leave every situation properly so that you enter properly. It is vital that you never leave any learning position prematurely for any reason as this will be your ingress into any new situation of leadership. A great leader never leads all the time as they are constantly learning from better leaders to increase their leadership skills and abilities.

 Practical application; this is the process in which the leader applies all that he or she has learned. I stated earlier that the wise person is one who applies knowledge; however the ignorant leader fails to apply knowledge to their lives. Walking in leadership is a continual learning curve and no matter how prepared one is there is always something new to learn; so practical application is an incessant process. Always remember the road to success is continuously under construction!

Being the leader you were called to be; is the very last one of these steps in ones evolution from follower to leader. It is ultimately a choice that one makes after going through these steps. Now my steps are not the only solution and or absolution for being the leader one is called to be. However, through my recipe for success over the years it has allowed leadership to manifest itself through me by following these steps. Many have the call to leadership but only a few choose to answer the call. Be the one who answers such a call so that our world, our states, our cities, and our communities have great leaders to follow. You may ask why should you be the one to lead and my answer is; Why not you, and why not now?

Conclusion

To move forward after receiving information is truly a choice. The average individual will receive information and typically loose it expediently. They will lose it not because they are irresponsible, or unappreciative of the opportunity they were given to receive such information, but because they did not put it to action. It is very easy to receive information and loose it because of the lack of practical application of information. If wisdom is applied knowledge then ignorance is unused knowledge and we never want to misuse knowledge. There are a lot of wise individuals out there but twice as many ignorant individuals simply because they are not applying knowledge that has been given to them. I want to stop the level of ignorance in this world and empower people with information.

The exclusive purpose of this book is to equip its reader with knowledge on leadership and practical ways to walk in such leadership. My sincere hope is that this will challenge the reader to strive to be the best leader they are capable of being. I have heard people say things like so and so is a "natural born leader", and this is true to a certain extent. The real truth is that people are either born with a natural instinct to lead or they aren't. If you are one who was not born with that natural instinct then this book is sure to help you cultivate such characteristics. This absolutely will not happen if you do not apply the information given in the first two chapters. The information provided has been applied for years, practiced for many years as well and is proven leadership material. No, this is not a money back guarantee type of book but one that is sure to work because it is sound information.

In addition this book was written to encourage as well as motivate those who have aspirations of becoming leaders. It was also written to inspire those who may feel like it is too late to develop this attribute that turns into their character. WE as a society lack in the areas of leadership today in 2015. This is not to say that there are no leaders out there but really to bring light to the lack thereof. In my many years of mentoring and coaching I have come across many people who simply don't lead and there are many different reasons why. Now of course these reasons vary from person to person and from situation to situation, too many to name in this book. The bottom line is that there are more who choose to follow over leading in my personal experience. I said this to say that I feel a deep conviction to empower people both young and old with knowledge that can help them to become strong leaders.

Leadership true enough is a decision one makes to walk in however, it there is information out there that helps ones decision to become a leader easier then why not provide such material. We as individuals in this world are a part of a giant puzzle that has to be put together and I feel my part is to build leaders. I have experienced many times over the lack of audacity in many individuals whether it was them being shy or them not being confident enough to lead. In either case I feel a strong desire to help bring out the leader within. I will use all avenues and opportunities to do so.

In my book Being a Leader of Leaders I discuss how important it is to lead by example and in this book I feel like I am doing that by providing this information. The best leader in my opinion is one who can take information, consume it, and successfully regurgitate it to others for maximum achievement. The nature of this subject is vital to the aspiring leader's success. Leadership as a whole is a subject that cannot just be talked about it must be explored and applied to one's life.

Here are a few things to remember for practical application of Leadership attributes and characteristics.

1. You have to be willing to be challenged after receiving information.

2. Understand that nothing comes easy especially something that will change your life for the better.
3. Leadership is a choice not a privilege handed to you.
4. Constantly be aware that there is grave responsibility that comes with the title leader.
5. Correct preparation results in you being cognizant of the fact that as your confidence grows as a leader your comfort zones will be challenged.
6. As you become more aware of your insecurities while growing in leadership they must be dealt with as they are revealed to you.
7. Prepare yourself because as you grow in leadership

that your life becomes more like fish bowls that everyone can look into, censure, judge, evaluate and give their opinions on or about.

8. Becoming a leader is uncomfortable but to go somewhere you've never gone you must do something you've never done.

9. Always be mindful that leadership is never to be taken lightly or devalued for any reason.

10. Huge success is waiting for those who understand the momentous responsibility that comes with being a leader.

So there you have it some practical ways to ensure your success as an inspiring leader. I have no doubt that when one applies these steps that there will be success and progress. Keeping in mind that leadership is constantly being developed through those who aspire to be great leaders.

The road to success is a constant road traveled and one never truly reaches a final destination while on this road. In addition to this the road to success is always under reconstruction. There are diversions, alterations, digressions, mishaps, accidents, challenges and valuable lessons learned on this road.

A true leader is ever learning, ever growing, inquisitive, enthusiastic, and never negates the opportunity to sharpen their leadership skills. They understand that the end goal is being a great leader and they remain focused on obtaining the dream of becoming and maintaining the role of a leader.

Everyone Has a Story

My Story

As a final thought I would like to share part of my life story as I want to encourage anyone who may feel like they don't have what it takes to become a great leader. There is a bible verse that I try to live my life by that says "if you have it within your means to help someone and close your heart to their need how does God's love abide in you!" (1 John 3:17). This verse expresses my desire to help people who are on their journey to greatness. There have been many challenges to my own individual journey and I feel it necessary to help others as they aspire to become great in their own right! I always like to take the opportunities given to me to share my story and here it is...

At an early age I was diagnosed with Macular Degeneration coupled with Star guard's disease. This (macular Degeneration) typically develops in individuals when they are older in age however, it happened to me at around age 8. This was pretty devastating as I grew older and began to look forward to things like driving, college, and becoming a mature, independent adult. I sat in doctor's office from age 8 until I was finally diagnosed in 1979. In the spring of 1980 I was told by doctors that at the rate my vision was leaving that I was going to be totally blind by age 16. I was completely speechless for a few minutes trying to take in what I was just told. I waited about 2 minutes and looked at my mother and said "I don't receive that!" I left that office to visit low vision specialists and Retinal specialists for months at a time. I received bad news after bad news never being encouraged to fight for my future and or success. I was told by one doctor not to plan a future, attaining a driver's license was completely out of the question, and college would be too high of an expectation. They told me bad news before they ever told me anything positive. I remember walking into one doctor's office and him telling me that I was a miracle and before he could take the words back I said "I know I am!" He just couldn't understand how I functioned so well based on the doctors reports he had examined.

As time when on I was not prepared by the schools to enter college as they felt it necessary to keep me in remedial courses that were less than college prep courses. I was rebellious at every request and requirement. I pushed to take higher classes and although I entered some it was too late as I began preparing for life as a young adult. I did everything they said or thought I could not do. I started working at age 14; I obtained a license, prepared for college, all while learning to use brail, trained to use a Seeing Eye dog, utilizing a blind man's cane, and learning how to use a multiplicity of visual aids. I had established enough fundamental courses to apply for colleges I did not think I would be accepted to. To my chagrin I was accepted to seven different colleges. I chose Tennessee State University and because of my unpreparedness I entered on academic probation as a result of low math scores, and average ACT scores.

After much hard work and a geographical change I obtained Leadership awards and commendations, an Associates and Bachelor's degree along with much more training as a leader. I became a coach and educator. I am now pursuing more education and fulfilling my dream as a writer. I want to encourage anyone who is reading this book to know that you can accomplish anything you set your mind to accomplish. Never let anyone or anything hinder you from pursuing your dreams no matter how far or unattainable they may appear. Nothing is impossible when you believe in yourself and have faith. In my situation I was pushed to leadership and had some great examples of leaders while growing up. I chose to reproduce what they instilled in me and over the years I have shared the wealth. I through this book and many to come will continue to do so.

Be strong and remain focused on all that you want to accomplish because it's never too late to reach your dreams!

-Denaryle Lovell Williams

www.ingramcontent.com/pod-product-compliance
Lightning Source LLC
Chambersburg PA
CBHW060032050426
42448CB00012B/2970